SLED RACING
DOGS

BY ALICIA Z. KLEPEIS

CANINE

★

ATHLETES

SportsZone

An Imprint of Abdo Publishing
abdobooks.com

abdobooks.com

Published by Abdo Publishing, a division of ABDO, PO Box 398166, Minneapolis, Minnesota 55439. Copyright © 2019 by Abdo Consulting Group, Inc. International copyrights reserved in all countries. No part of this book may be reproduced in any form without written permission from the publisher. SportsZone™ is a trademark and logo of Abdo Publishing.

Printed in the United States of America, North Mankato, Minnesota
092018
012019

THIS BOOK CONTAINS
RECYCLED MATERIALS

Cover Photo: iStockphoto
Interior Photos: Christian Bruna/EPA/REX/Shutterstock, 5; iStockphoto, 6, 25; Mark Thiessen/AP Images, 9; Winter and Pond/Library of Congress/Corbis/VCG/Getty Images, 11; Robert Bower/The Idaho Post-Register/AP Images, 13; Alexander Piragis/Shutterstock Images, 15; Natalia Fedosova/Shutterstock Images, 17; Andrew Milligan/PA Wire URN:25283039/Press Association/AP Images, 19, 26; Kirk Geisler/Shutterstock Images, 21; Michael Dinneen/AP Images, 23; Sergey Lavrentev/Shutterstock Images, 29

Editor: Marie Pearson
Series Designer: Craig Hinton
Library of Congress Control Number: 2018949089

Publisher's Cataloging-in-Publication Data

Names: Klepeis, Alicia Z., author.
Title: Sled racing dogs / by Alicia Z. Klepeis.
Description: Minneapolis, Minnesota : Abdo Publishing, 2019 | Series: Canine athletes | Includes online resources and index.
Identifiers: ISBN 9781532117411 (lib. bdg.) | ISBN 9781641855983 (pbk) | ISBN 9781532170270 (ebook)
Subjects: LCSH: Dog sports--Juvenile literature. | Sled dog racing--Juvenile literature. | Dogs--Behavior--Juvenile literature. | Sled dogs--Juvenile literature.
Classification: DDC 798.8--dc23

TABLE OF
CONTENTS

CHAPTER 1

ON THE TRAIL.............................. 4

CHAPTER 2

HOW SLED DOG RACING STARTED.....10

CHAPTER 3

BREEDS AND TRAINING 16

CHAPTER 4

BASICS OF SLED DOG RACING........ 22

GLOSSARY 30

MORE INFORMATION................................. 31

ONLINE RESOURCES 31

INDEX.. 32

ABOUT THE AUTHOR 32

ON THE TRAIL

It's a frigid March day in central Alaska. Teams of sled dogs are barking wildly. They are ready to run. It takes nearly a dozen people to keep them from dashing onto the trail.

A young musher looks over her team of dogs one last time. She makes sure their harnesses are in place. She checks that the towline is connected properly to the harnesses and to the sled. She gives each of her eight Alaskan huskies a scratch behind the ears.

Sled dogs are wild with excitement at the beginning of a race.

Sled dogs take off at the beginning of the race.

A race official gives the musher the signal. It's her turn to set off. The musher tells her helpers that it's time to let go of the towline. She takes a deep breath and yells, "Hike!"

The dogs are off in a flash. Thirty-two booted paws sprint away from the start line. The wind whips snow all around.

Minutes later, the team is far away from the sights and sounds of the city. The two lead dogs, Willow and Jasper, set the pace for the team. They also keep their fellow team dogs on the trail.

Up ahead is a frozen lake. The trail veers off to the left. The musher calls out "Haw!" This command tells the dogs to turn left. The snow whooshes as the team makes a fast but smooth turn. The dogs do not bark when running. The path is quiet, except for the dogs' footsteps crunching in the snow and the swoosh of the sled.

The young racer and her sled dog team travel for many miles and days. But her sled is full of supplies and food. Her team has been training for this race for months. They stop at checkpoints along the way to rest, eat, and sleep.

The trail is challenging. They run into a patch of ice, and one dog gets a cut on his paw. He is dropped from the race, and an airplane picks him up and brings him to safety. One evening, a swirling snowstorm makes it almost impossible to see. If it hadn't been for the watchful lead dogs, the team might have lost the trail completely. Good lead dogs will lead the team away from danger, even if it goes against the musher's command.

But finally the musher and her team cross the finish line in good time. She doesn't win but is thrilled to have completed the race. She is proud of her dogs' enthusiasm for racing.

WHAT IS SLED DOG RACING?

Sled dog racing is an action-packed, exciting sport. The canine athletes that participate in this sport are finely tuned running and pulling machines. Pound for pound, sled racing dogs are even stronger than horses. Mushers act as the coaches, and the dogs as the athletes.

Sled racing dogs take on terrain that would intimidate most human runners. They cross vast stretches of tundra. They zoom past trees and fly easily along trails over frozen lakes. They have been known to hit top speeds of nearly 30 miles per hour (48 km/h) when sprinting. Sled racing dogs are powerful athletes.

DANGERS ON THE TRAIL

Sled dogs encounter many potential dangers while racing. Frostbite is one. Another is cutting their paws on jagged ice or rough ground. Racing dogs can suffer from exhaustion due to all the energy used when racing. These dangers make it important that mushers know their dogs and when to pull one from a race.

Crowds gather to cheer on the teams as they cross the finish line.

HOW SLED DOG RACING STARTED

Today sled dog racing is a well-organized sport. But people used sled dogs long before the modern races began. Originally people used sled dogs for transportation, not for sport. Dogsleds carried both people and their belongings. Archaeologists believe dogs were first used to pull sleds in Siberia thousands of years ago.

In the North American Arctic, indigenous communities also used sled dogs. The Inuit of northern Canada, Alaska, and Greenland have used sled dogs for thousands

Dogs and sleds have long been used to transport people and supplies.

of years. The US Postal Service even used sled dog teams to carry the mail in Alaska until the 1960s.

EARLY HISTORY OF THE SPORT

Experts debate exactly when the sport of sled dog racing began. Some people think informal races were held during the Gold Rush in Alaska in the late 1890s. Groups of dogsledders got together to see whose teams were strongest and fastest. In 1907 the Nome Kennel Club formed and a year later held its first official competition, the All Alaska Sweepstakes. The race, which is no longer held, went from Nome to Candle and back to Nome, a distance of 408 miles (657 km).

The oldest race still being run in the United States is the American Dog Derby. It began in 1917. The first race ran from West Yellowstone, Montana, to Ashton, Idaho. Today the American Dog Derby includes five different races.

It seems that Alaska was the birthplace for sled dog racing. But races have grown in number in both the United States and Canada since the early 1900s. Sled dog racing

The American Dog Derby races travel across farmland.

was also part of Europe's sporting culture for much of the 1900s. Scandinavians have held official competitions for almost 70 years.

THE SPORT TODAY

Sled dog racing has grown in popularity since its early days. Today races are held in several US states. Racers also compete in several countries around the globe, including Canada, Norway, Sweden, and Russia.

One of the world's most famous races is the Iditarod. This race takes place in Alaska. The Iditarod was started in part as a way to preserve dogsledding culture. This race has grown each year since it began in 1973.

There are also sled dog races for kids. The Jr. Iditarod is one. Mushers can be between 14 and 17 years old. The race is 150 miles (240 km) long. That's like traveling from the eastern border of Rhode Island to the western border of Connecticut.

People get excited about sled dog racing for many reasons. For some it's the thrill of speed. For others it's a great way to enjoy the outdoors. Like any sport, there's also the excitement of competition.

Many sled dog racers join clubs that promote the sport. There are sled dog clubs across the country. Clubs often organize races. The North Star Sled Dog Club (NSSDC) runs

WOMEN AND THE IDITAROD

In 1985 Libby Riddles became the first woman to win the Iditarod. She and her 13-dog team fought through horrendous blizzards to cross the finish line first. A woman named Susan Butcher won the next three Iditarods. In 1987 Butcher won with a record-breaking time. She finished in 11 days, 2 hours, and 5 minutes.

Sled dog racing isn't just for adults. Some clubs host races for children and teenagers.

several races. These races take place in Minnesota, Iowa, Wisconsin, North Dakota, and the Canadian provinces of Ontario and Manitoba.

BREEDS AND TRAINING

Any big dog can pull a sled. But some breeds are used more than others. The most common racing dogs are the Siberian husky and Alaskan husky.

Siberian huskies are lightweight and strong. Their compact bodies are terrific at pulling relatively light loads quickly over long distances. These dogs have a dense, two-layered coat that helps them tolerate extreme cold. Their bodies burn fat at different rates depending on how hard they are working. This allows them to travel long distances without wearing out.

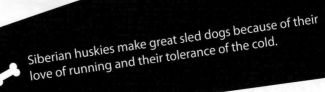 Siberian huskies make great sled dogs because of their love of running and their tolerance of the cold.

The Alaskan husky is the most commonly used sled dog. Alaskan huskies are not a breed but a type of dog. They began as a mix of Siberian huskies, hounds such as greyhounds, and pointers such as German shorthaired pointers. They are bred for working ability, not looks. Alaskan huskies are leaner and larger than Siberian huskies. These dogs are designed for hauling and racing. Alaskan huskies can pull hundreds of pounds of cargo and people through the snow. They can run 100 miles (160 km) per day for many days in a row.

Regardless of breed, all sled dogs have an unquenchable desire to run. They must also have healthy appetites. They have to eat whatever is given to them on the trail. Sled dogs must have tough feet. Any racecourse can include rough ground or jagged ice.

TRAINING SLED RACING DOGS

Sled dogs start training as puppies. Trainers handle puppies shortly after birth. It's important for puppies to get used to being around people. As the puppies get

Trainers handle sled dog puppies a lot so the puppies learn to behave when preparing for a race.

older, they start interacting with other dogs. They also learn to come when their trainers call them.

There are different ways of training sled dogs. But all mushers must make sure the training is fun for their puppies. At a couple of months old, a puppy starts training by wearing a collar and harness. It gets used to the feel of such equipment. As the puppy grows, the trainer will attach an object to the rope hanging from the harness. This could be a piece of wood or a tire. The weight attached to this rope will increase as the dog grows. To a sled dog puppy, this is like a game. The puppy might pull the weight for approximately 100 feet (30 m). Before running in a harness, the pups might be encouraged to chase all-terrain vehicles. At approximately one year old, dogs start running attached to a sled.

PRACTICE MAKES PERFECT

Sled dogs practice a lot as a team before they're ready to race. The mushers make sure the dogs get along and obey commands. The dogs also must be strong and fast enough to be successful competitors.

At first a young dog might be part of a small team of perhaps four to six dogs, which could include its mother and some siblings. Over time, if the dog seems content with pulling for a short distance, the musher will increase the distance. Eventually the dog will be conditioned to pull a sled with a bigger team. Dogs in training may run thousands of miles per year. They do both short- and long-distance runs. By the time trained sled dogs are two years old, they're ready to race.

IT TAKES A TEAM

Every sled dog on a racing team has its own role to play. Lead dogs are in the front of a sled dog team.

WHEEL DOGS — TEAM DOGS — SWING DOGS — LEAD DOGS

Each dog has an important role on a sled team.

They must follow the musher's commands. They set the pace and make sure the whole team is heading in the right direction. Lead dogs must be smart and have good hearing. They can't be easily distracted.

Swing dogs are right behind the lead dogs. They help turn the team right or left. Some mushers use the swing dog position to train future lead dogs. Team dogs are between the swing dogs and the wheel dogs. They help maintain the team's speed. Team dogs are the muscle of the team. Wheel dogs are the last dogs in a sled dog team. They both pull and steer the sled. Talented wheel dogs know how to help guide the sled around obstacles such as trees.

BASICS OF SLED DOG RACING

There are different types of sled dog races. In a sprint race, dogsled teams cover short distances at top speed. A sprint race could be 5 miles (8 km) long. The dogs might be running 20 to 25 miles per hour (32–40 km/h). By comparison, dogs might run at 6 to 7.5 miles per hour (9.7–12 km/h) in distance races.

Distance races come in many lengths. Mid-range races often go up to 200 miles (320 km). But the Iditarod is more than 1,000 miles (1,600 km). It truly tests a dog's endurance.

Sled dog racing isn't all work.
Mushers also take time to bond with their dogs.

SLEDS AND OTHER SUPPLIES

Many supplies are needed for sled dog racing. The sled itself is one. Today's mushers commonly use high-tech sleds. These must be strong and durable yet lightweight. They are often made from aluminum or similar metals.

Basket sleds are most common for racing. A flat-bedded basket rises above the sled's two runners. Since the basket is above the level of the snow, the musher's equipment inside stays dry.

The musher stands on top of runners in the back of the sled. The runners are like skis. They're often made of plastic. Racers may wax the runners just like skiers do. This keeps them running smoothly over the trail.

An important part of racing sleds is the brake system. The brake system is mounted onto the back end of a sled. It's usually made up of a spring-loaded wooden plank on one side and a metal hook or plate on the other. On the trail, a musher steps on the brake to slow the sled down.

PARTS OF
A SLED

HANDLE BAR

BASKET

BRUSH BOW

RUNNER

Whether competing or training, mushers should regularly check their dogs for injury.

Mushers need lots of supplies for racing. Comfortable harnesses for their dogs are important. Harnesses help capture energy from the team. Racers may use booties to protect their dogs' paws. Mushers may also bring dog jackets. These can keep dogs warm when traveling in frigid temperatures or when the dogs are resting at night.

Mushers always bring food for themselves and their dogs. Depending on the race, mushers often bring additional supplies. These can include an ax and snowshoes, used in case mushers have to break trail in a race; a cold weather sleeping bag; a cooker and pot for boiling water; fuel to bring water to a boil; extra booties for each dog; and a veterinarian notebook, which must be presented to a veterinarian at each checkpoint. The vet must examine each dog and sign off on their health in the book before a team can continue the race.

RULES OF COMPETITION

Just like human races, sled dog races have rules. Sometimes teams have to run one or more qualifying races before entering an official race. This is the case for those wanting to compete in the Iditarod. Racers must prove they can handle traveling through the wilderness and that their dogs are properly cared for and prepared.

After teams have qualified for a long race, mushers ship food and supplies to various checkpoints along the route. It would be impossible to carry the weight of supplies needed for some races.

Shortly before race day, mushers must gather certain medical paperwork. This shows that their dogs have been vaccinated, for example. Some races require that all dogs have a microchip embedded under their skin. This allows people to keep track of their team members with a computer.

Each race has rules about how many dogs may be on a team. It might be that eight to 12 dogs must start the race but only six must finish. Dogs can't be added to a team once the race has begun.

To start the race, a musher is given a signal. Teams are staggered by at least two minutes. That way, each team has space to start running. Once on the trail, mushers must follow lots of rules. Longer races have mandatory stops or checkpoints along the route. This allows the teams to rest. Veterinarians can examine the dogs to be sure they're healthy enough to continue racing. If a dog is injured or unwell, race rules typically require that a musher's sled carry those dogs. They may be flown to safety if necessary.

The winner of a sled dog race is the team that crosses the finish line first. The bigger sled dog races have cash prizes. The winner of the 2018 Iditarod won more than

OTHER SLED DOG SPORTS

Many other sports are similar to sled dog racing. Any healthy dog can enjoy them. Skijoring is when a dog or a team of dogs pulls a person wearing cross-country skis. And bikejoring is similar, except the dog pulls someone on a bicycle.

No snow? No problem! Trainers can keep their dogs in top shape by having them pull carts. There are even competitions for carts.

$50,000 and a new truck. Winners of some sled dog races get trophies as prizes.

Every sled dog race is challenging and exciting. Races show just how athletic sled dogs can be.

GLOSSARY

endurance
The ability to travel long distances.

frostbite
Injury to body tissues resulting from exposure to extreme cold.

harness
A set of straps or fittings used to fasten a sled dog to a sled.

hauling
Pulling a heavy load.

microchip
A tiny computer chip implanted under the skin of an animal. It contains a unique number that can be scanned and read to identify the dog.

musher
Someone who travels over snow on a sled pulled by dogs.

qualifying
Becoming eligible to participate in a competition after meeting a certain standard.

towline
A rope or cable that runs between the dogs on a team and connects them to the sled.

tundra
A large, flat, treeless plain found in the Arctic regions of North America, Europe, and Asia.

MORE INFORMATION

ONLINE RESOURCES

To learn more about sled racing dogs, visit **abdobooklinks.com**. These links are routinely monitored and updated to provide the most current information available.

BOOKS

Furstinger, Nancy. *Dogs*. Minneapolis, MN: Abdo Publishing, 2014.

Hamilton, John. *Alaska: The Last Frontier*. Minneapolis, MN: Abdo Publishing, 2017.

Hamilton, S. L. *Iditarod*. Minneapolis, MN: Abdo Publishing, 2013.

INDEX

Alaska, 4, 10–12, 14

Alaskan huskies, 4, 16–18

American Dog Derby, 12

bikejoring, 28

Butcher, Susan, 14

distance races, 22

Iditarod, 14, 22, 27, 28

    Jr. Iditarod, 14

Inuit, 10

mushers, 8, 14, 19–21

Nome Kennel Club, 12

North Star Sled Dog
    Club, 14

Postal Service, US, 12

prizes, 28–29

Riddles, Libby, 14

rules, 27–28

safety, 7, 8, 26–27, 28

Scandinavians, 13

Siberia, 10

Siberian huskies, 16–18

skijoring, 28

sprint races, 22

supplies, 24–27

teams, 20–21

    lead dogs, 6, 7,
      20–21

training, 18–20

ABOUT THE AUTHOR

Alicia Z. Klepeis began her career at the National Geographic Society. A former middle school teacher, she is the author of numerous children's books including *Trolls*, *Snakes Are Awesome*, *Haunted Cemeteries Around the World*, and *A Time for Change*. Alicia hopes to see the Iditarod race in person someday.